Yvan's Workshop
Sandwiches and Then Some

Yvan's Workshop
Sandwiches and Then Some

/ Recipes: Yvan Cadiou /
/ Photographs: Jean-Pierre and Valentin Duval /
/ Recipe editing and lay-out: Marie-Alexandre Perraud and Muriel Villebrun /
/ Translation: Anne Trager /

Romain Pages Publishing

Sandwiches with a French touch!

Every day, throughout the world, millions of sandwiches get gobbled up, for lack of time, or out of habit. People often choose sandwiches because they have a limited budget, sometimes by gourmet inclination, but rarely in a creative quest. I, personally, will admit to moments of gluttony. (When I was a child, I dreamed of raiding the refrigerator. At the time, my dear mother Yvette used to say, "Your eyes are bigger than your stomach." She was right. I was very fond of food, and always filching things in the pantry!) And for me, a sandwich break can be a real culinary adventure!

I come from a working class background, where sandwiches were considered a reward for hard work, often representing an entire meal, or at least a hearty snack. Most of the time, they were made with two large slices of bread that held together all sorts of foodstuffs. They came out on many occasions: during breaks where my father was building his sailboat, for work done in the garden or the garage, for a picnic on the beach, at day camp, and at holiday camp, just to name a few.

My younger brother Philippe, a designer who deals in second hand goods, has lived in Paris for a good number of years, and is a huge adept of sandwiches, which seriously lack variety. For a long time, I have promised to help him eat a better diet, which inspired a number of ideas for sandwiches of all sorts. My goal was to provide a variety of shapes and flavours, both originality and balance. So I decided to share these ideas with all the young and less young who have had enough of the sad, oh-so-banal ham sandwich, and who dream of a little happiness and some taste tantalizing.

In France, you find café-counter sandwiches, and in recent years, working class bistros have returned from the mist of the distant past. A number of restaurants, cafés, bistros and brasseries have taken on a new style of very trendy sandwich, both with two slices and open face. The rest of the world did not wait for France to catch up. The Dutch are champions in the matter; Scandinavia, Italy, America, Britain and the countries around the Mediterranean all have their specialties.

My goal is to offer a selection of sandwiches with a French touch, cooked with pleasure and which give more than a fair share to bread and flavour blends. These are simple, friendly encounters for food lovers and easy on the wallet. They can be eaten with others, or alone. They represent a passion for cooking accessible to everyone and that includes *Sandwiches and Then Some*, a portable cuisine for home and street eating.

Yvan Cadiou, taste sculptor

Notes: Each recipe is classified with a few keywords, found on the right page, which give the following information: the type of sandwich, an indication of its size, and its main ingredient. From the pictures, some of these snacks may seem hard to transport. We tried to make them attractive, to whet your appetite with the contents rather than simply present a top slice of bread. Of course, you can adapt the size to bring them on picnics, or to carry your ideal sandwich for your lunch break. We often present the open face sandwiches in layers: the number depends on how hungry you are!

Recipes

/ Sea Scallop Canapés, Borneo Style /

Preparation: 20 minutes

Ingredients

- 20 small slices round white bread, or 40 to make tea sandwiches
- 6 or 7 sea scallops
- 6 or 7 bamboo shoots
- 1 ripe banana
- 1 or 2 tomatoes
- 40 g/2⅔ tablespoons softened butter (or mayonnaise)
- a few sprigs fresh coriander (cilantro)
- juice of ½ lemon
- 1 dash soy sauce
- a few drops sesame oil
- olive oil
- white pepper

If you buy whole sea scallops, shell them, remove the beard and the coral (you can save the latter for another preparation). Wash the scallops by placing them in a large quantity of water and lifting them out, three times, without soaking them. Cut the scallops into two or three round slices. Sprinkle with lemon juice and olive oil, add a dash of soy sauce and pepper. Marinate a few minutes.

Wash the coriander leaves and the tomatoes. Chop a few sprigs of coriander. Cut the tomatoes into very thin slices and then into short sticks. Cut the bamboos shoots into thin slices. Peel the banana and cut into thin slices.

Toast the bread slices and butter them lightly. Spread each with the chopped coriander, add a few slices of bamboo shoots, one or two banana slices and a piece of scallop. Sprinkle with a few drops of sesame oil. Decorate with a few sticks of tomato and a coriander leaf.

For the small sandwich version, proceed in the same way, reducing the quantities and adding another piece of toast to top it off.

/ Borneo is an island in Southeast Asia. Bamboo shoots and the delicate taste of soy sauce are reminiscent of the flavours found there. /

x 4

/ Swede on Wasa /

Preparation: 35 minutes
Cooking time: 20 minutes

Ingredients

- 12 pieces Wasa crispbread
- 400 g/14 oz fresh pink shrimp
  (or cooked and frozen)
- 2 potatoes, preferably untreated
- 1 generous handful mixed greens
- 1 cucumber
- 4 cherry tomatoes
- 1 lemon
- 2 or 3 large sweet pickles
  or pickled vegetables
- olive oil
- salt and white pepper

Scandinavian mayonnaise:
- 1 egg yolk, at room temperature
- 1 teaspoon mustard
- 1 teaspoon honey
- a little fresh dill (optional)
- 15 to 20 cl/5 fl oz/³/₅ to ⁴/₅ cup
  sunflower oil
- a few drops vinegar
- salt and white pepper

Mix the egg yolk, mustard and vinegar. Season with salt and pepper. Add the oil little by little, whisking constantly to make the mayonnaise. Add the honey and a little chopped fresh dill (optional). If you are using fresh shrimp, drop them into boiling salted water, bring back to a boil, drain and shell. If they are frozen, allow them to thaw slowly to room temperature and then shell them.

Cook the potatoes in boiling salted water for 15 to 20 minutes. Peel them first if they are treated. Wash the cucumber and cut into thin slices. Cut the potatoes into small pieces and mix them delicately with a little mayonnaise.

Wash the mixed greens. Place a few leaves on a plate. Top with a piece of Wasa crispbread and spread with a little mayonnaise. Add a few cucumber slices, a few shrimp and another Wasa, potatoes, mayonnaise and shrimp. Top with a last piece of Wasa, garnished with cucumber slices, shrimp, a touch of mayonnaise and a leaf of lettuce. Decorate this piled up open sandwich with a cherry tomato and a piece of pickle. Season with a little salt and pepper. Add two lemon sections to the plate, and sprinkle with a dash of olive oil.

/ This slightly sweet, dill-flavoured Scandinavian mayonnaise goes well with the Wasa. /

x 2

/ Norway–Morocco Express /

Preparation: 25 minutes
Cooking time: 20 minutes

Ingredients

- 1 round semolina bread
- 100 g/3½ oz smoked salmon
- 100 to 120 g/3½ to 4¼ oz cream cheese
- 1 aubergine (eggplant)
- 1 large tomato or a few cherry tomatoes
- 1 lettuce heart
- a few young spinach leaves
- 1 bunch coriander leaves (cilantro)
- dried basil or other dried herb
- juice of ½ orange
- juice of ½ lemon
- olive oil
- salt and white pepper

Preheat the oven to 240°C/475°F/gas 9. Wash the aubergine and cut lengthwise into somewhat thick strips. Place them on a baking dish, sprinkle with olive oil, season with salt and add a pinch of dried basil. Bake for about 20 minutes, or until the strips are well grilled.

Cut the aubergine strips into rough pieces. Season with orange juice, a dash of lemon juice and a bit of olive oil. Add salt, pepper and the chopped coriander leaves. Marinate a few minutes.

Wash the lettuce and spinach. Cut the bread into two pieces lengthwise, open and spread with cream cheese. Top with some lettuce leaves and raw spinach leaves, add the aubergine, a little of the sauce and the smoked salmon. Insert tomato slices in the salmon.

Add coriander leaves, pepper, a dash of olive oil and, if you want, a touch more cream cheese. Sprinkle the inside of the sandwich tops with the rest of the marinade and then cover the sandwich.

/ Semolina bread recipes vary depending on which country around the Mediterranean they come from (Morocco, Lebanon, and Turkey, for example). You can find a variety of them in Arab specialty shops. Choose one with a good-sized soft part. /

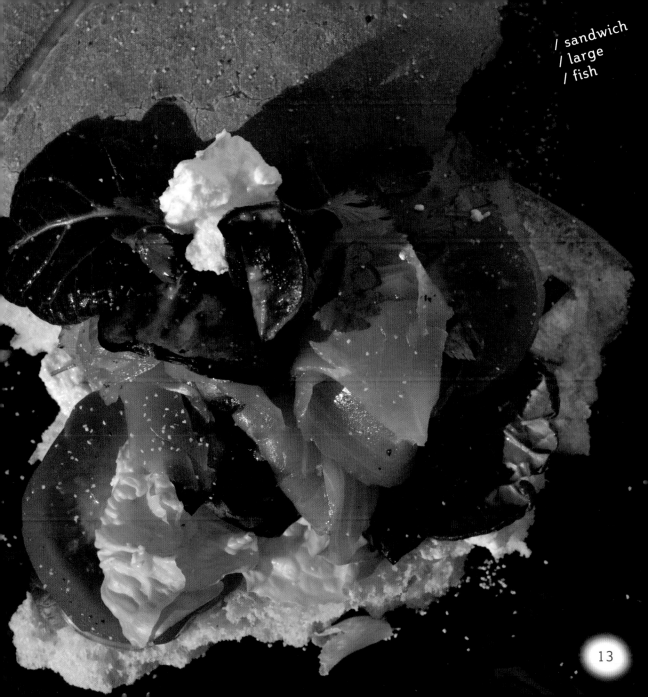

13

x 1

/ Borneo Turkey Roll /

Preparation: 20 minutes
Cooking time: 15 minutes

Ingredients

- 1 small round bread roll
- 150 g/5¼ oz turkey fillet
- 1 potato
- 1 shallot or small onion
- 1 small apple
- ½ banana
- 1 small fresh chilli (optional)
- 1 tablespoon grated coconut
  + 2 pinches for decoration
- 1 handful almonds, cashews
  or peanuts
- 1 teaspoon of each of the following
  spices: curry powder, ground coriander seeds, curcuma, ground cumin
- 1 teaspoon sesame oil
- 1 tablespoon sunflower oil
- olive oil
- salt

Peel the potato and cut it into a small dice. Peel the shallot, chop finely and mix with the potato. Heat the sunflower and sesame oils in a skillet, add the spices, grated coconut and almonds and cook over high heat for 1 minute. Slice the turkey and brown over high heat with the spices and the chilli, cut into very small pieces. After 3 minutes, add the potatoes and the shallot. Cook for another 3 minutes, sprinkle with a small glass of water and season with salt. Cover and cook over medium heat for 7 to 8 minutes.

Peel the banana and the apple, dice and mix. Cut off the top of the round bread and remove the soft inside. Garnish the inside with the cooked preparation, adding the raw fruit. Douse with olive oil and sprinkle lightly with grated coconut.

x 4

/ Algerian-style Pan Bagnat /

Preparation: 25 minutes
Cooking time: 9 minutes

Ingredients

- 4 small round bread rolls
- 150 g/5¼ oz tuna (canned, natural, or fresh and cooked)
- 2 eggs
- 1 or 2 tomatoes
- 4 dried tomatoes marinated in olive oil
- 4 cherry tomatoes
- ½ cucumber
- 1 dozen pitted green olives
- a few pickled vegetables
- a few pickled chillies
- 1 teaspoon harissa spice paste (optional)
- a few sprigs of coriander leaves (cilantro)
- juice of ½ lemon
- olive oil
- salt

Hard boil the egg in boiling water for 9 minutes. Refresh under cold water and then peel. Cut open the bread rolls. Wash the tomatoes, grate them, add a dash of olive oil, the harissa (optional) to taste, and season with salt and pepper. Mix well. Spread the sandwich bottoms with this tomato mixture.

Peel the cucumber and cut it into tagliatelle-like strips using a vegetable peeler. Add a little cucumber and crumbled tuna onto the sandwich. Cut the pickled vegetables into small pieces and add with the chopped dried tomatoes and a few olives. Cut the eggs into quarters and place two on each sandwich. Add a cherry tomato, strips of the chilli and a few coriander leaves. Sprinkle with a dash of olive oil and lemon juice.

17

x 2 to 4

/ Artichoke Heart Challah /

Preparation: 30 minutes
Cooking time: 15 minutes

Ingredients

- 1 large challah (Sabbath bread)
- 4 artichokes
- 50 g/1¾ oz/½ cup feta
- 2 handfuls pine nuts
- 2 to 4 hard-boiled quail eggs (available already cooked and peeled in jars)
- 1 small sweet onion
- 1 tomato
- 1 lettuce heart
- 2 lemons
- 1 small bunch parsley
- 1 tablespoon flour
- 2 small glasses white vinegar
- olive oil
- salt and pepper

Mix the flour with a little water, add to 1 litre/1¾ pts salted water with a glass of white vinegar, and bring to a boil. This will be used to cook the artichokes without colouring them.

Rub your hands with lemon juice so they won't be stained when you prepare the artichoke hearts. Break off the stem of the artichoke with the palm of your hand. Cut off the leaves, turning the artichoke to get remove the leaves on all sides (in French, this technique is called "turning" the artichoke). Make sure you remove the dark green bitter part. Use a vegetable peeler to even out the heart. Slide a knife in just at the level of the choke to remove the cone of small, tender leaves. Rub the entire heart with lemon juice and place in a large boil of water with added vinegar. Repeat the operation with the other artichokes. Cook the artichokes in the boiling water, vinegar and flour mixture, at a simmer for 15 minutes until they are tender. Refresh under cold water. Carefully remove the choke with your fingertips.

Grill the pine nuts in the oven. Cut one artichoke heart into pieces and place in a mortar. Add half of the feta, the chopped parsley and half of the pine nuts. Season with salt and pepper. Crush using a pestle, add a little olive oil at a time until you get a thick paste. Add the juice of a half a lemon and mix well.

Wash the lettuce and tomato. Peel the onion. Thinly slice the onion, tomato and remaining artichokes. Cut open the bread lengthwise and spread the bottom with the artichoke paste. Top with onion, lettuce, tomato and artichoke slices. Season with salt and pepper, add a dash of olive oil and a sprinkle of lemon juice. Sprinkle with crumbled feta and parsley leave. Add the remaining pine nuts and the quail eggs cut in half.

/ Challah, or Sabbath bread, can be found in specialty stores and is traditionally served on the Jewish Sabbath. You can also use a braided brioche bread. /

/ A cooking "blanc" ("white"), which is made by adding flour and vinegar or lemon juice to water, preserves the vegetable's colour and structure during the cooking process. /

x 4

/ Paris–New York Deli Special /

Preparation: 20 minutes

Ingredients

- 4 small bread rolls
- 200 to 250 g/7 to 9 oz sliced pastrami
- 150 g/5¼ oz cream cheese
- 1 small courgette (zucchini)
- 1 to 2 carrots
- 2 large pickles
- 1 small bunch parsley
- 4 teaspoons mustard
- juice of 1 lemon
- olive oil
- salt and white pepper

Peel the carrots and grate them (medium grater). Wash the courgette and slice into strips using a vegetable peeler. Marinate the strips in lemon juice with a tablespoon of olive oil, the chopped parsley, salt and pepper.

Cut the bread rolls open lengthwise. Spread the bottom with the cream cheese and add a touch of mustard. Top with grated carrot, marinated courgette and pastrami slices. Add pickle slices. Douse with the rest of the marinade and a dash of olive oil. Pepper.

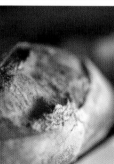

/ Pastrami is made from beef brisket. The meat is dipped into a thick brine and then smoked. Sometimes it is larded with green pepper corns or seasoned with coriander and pepper. /

x 2

/ Lebanese Wrap
for My Friend Ramzi /

Preparation: 20 minutes

Ingredients

- 1 small flat bread of your choice (pita, lavash, naan)
- 150 g/5¼ oz hummus
- 100 to 150 g/3½ to 5¼ oz/1½ to 2 cups cooked red or fava beans
- 100 to 150 g/3½ to 5¼ oz/1½ to 2 cups cooked chickpeas
- 3 small shallots
- 2 to 3 cloves garlic
- 1 generous handful of mixed greens
- 1 small bunch fresh coriander leaves (cilantro) or parsley
- 1 lemon
- 1 pinch ground cumin
- olive oil
- salt and white pepper

Wash the salad. Peel the shallots and the garlic cloves. Roughly chop up two shallots and crush them in a mortar with the garlic and a few coriander leaves. Add the salt, a pinch of cumin, a dash of lemon juice and a generous dash of olive oil. Spread this mixture onto the flatbread. Add hummus, chickpeas, red beans and a few salad leaves. Sprinkle with a dash of lemon and add a little finely chopped shallot and coriander leaves. Season with pepper. Roll the whole thing up before serving. Serve with lemon quarters.

/ To prepare the hummus, blend 150 g/5¼ oz/2 cups cooked chickpeas with a little tahini (sesame paste) or olive oil. Add a little orange and lemon juice, until you get a smooth spread. Season to taste with salt, pepper and chilli. /

x 1

/ Delta Trading Post /

Preparation: 15 minutes
Cooking time: 15 minutes

Ingredients

- 1 panini roll
- 1 small handful crayfish, precooked and shelled
- 3 green asparagus
- 1 large tomato
- 1 small sweet onion
- 1 handful rocket
- a few slices of pickled ginger (Asian specialty stores)
- a few sprigs of parsley
- juice of 1 lemon
- olive oil
- salt and pepper

Cut off the hard part of the asparagus stems, and peel the rest. Cook them for a few minutes either in a steamer or in boiling water. Keep them slightly al dente.

Put the precooked and shelled crayfish in a bowl with a dash of olive oil. Season with salt and pepper. Cut the asparagus into thin slices. Peel the onion and dice. Roughly chop the parsley and pickled ginger. Add all these ingredients to the crayfish and mix well. Wash the rocket and add half to the crayfish mixture. Sprinkle with lemon juice and toss.

Cut open the panini roll. Garnish with the prepared mixture, and sprinkle with olive oil. Close the sandwich with the top and cook in a panini or sandwich press for about 7 minutes. Serve with the remaining salad and the tomato cut into thin slices, seasoned with lemon juice, olive oil, salt and pepper.

/ If you want crisscrossed grill lines on the sandwich, think about turning it halfway through the cooking process. I created this sandwich in homage to the Comptoir du Delta (Delta Trading Post) which sells crayfish from the Camargue. /

x 2

/ Vegies, British Style /

Preparation: 25 minutes

Ingredients

- 1 barley baguette
- 1 small fennel bulb
- 1 or 2 large mushrooms,
  very white and firm
- 3 large tomatoes
- ½ courgette (zucchini)
- 1 shallot
- 4 dried tomatoes marinated in olive oil
- 2 or 3 tablespoons cooked chickpeas
- a few leaves curly endive
- a few sprigs parsley
- juice of ½ lemon
- olive oil
- salt and pepper

Wash the fennel bulb and cut it into slices with a mandoline. Remove the stems from the mushrooms and slice the caps thinly. Marinate the mushrooms and the fennel with a good dash of olive oil, a sprinkle of lemon juice, salt and pepper. Wash and chop the parsley. Chop the dried tomatoes finely. Add both parsley and tomatoes to the marinade. Wash the courgette and cut into round slices using the mandoline. Peel the shallot and chop finely. Wash the curly endive and the tomatoes.

Cut the baguette into two and then each piece lengthwise. Grate half a tomato onto each open sandwich and spread the tomato pulp onto the bread. Sprinkle with a dash of olive oil and add a few leaves of curly endive and a few courgette slices. Divide up the marinated vegetables and shallot between the sandwiches, and add a few chickpeas and tomato slices.

/ This sandwich is entirely vegetarian and invigorating, like something you can find in small trendy organic restaurants so common in Britain. /

/ The mandoline is a kitchen tool with an adjustable blade that allows you to choose what thickness you want. It also has other blades for other kinds of cuts, such as a julienne (thin sticks). /

/ Caribbean Chicken on Toast /

Preparation: 30 minutes
Cooking time: 10 minutes

Ingredients

- 20 small slices white bread
- 2 small chicken breasts
- 2 avocados
- 4 small tomatoes
- 4 slices of pickled ginger
  (Asian specialty stores)
- stems of 1 small bunch parsley
- 1 generous tablespoon Caribbean
  curry powder
- olive oil
- salt and black pepper

Heat a small cast-iron pot. Roll the chicken breasts in the Caribbean curry powder. Seize them without any fat, browning on both side, and then cook them over a low heat, uncovered, for 8 minutes.

Toast the bread slices. Remove the crust if you wish. Finely chop the pickled ginger. Wash the tomatoes and cut them into thin slices and then into a small dice. Wash the parsley stems and chop finely. Mix together the ginger, tomato and parsley.

Cut the chicken into thin slices, diagonally. Cut the avocados in half, and use a spoon to form generous shavings to place on the toast. Add the tomato mixture and one or two slices of chicken. Top with a little more of the tomato mixture for decoration. Season with salt and pepper and sprinkle with a few drops of olive oil.

/ Blackening is a traditionally Cajun cooking method that does not use cooking fat. It gives the chicken a smoky flavour and keeps it very tender. /

/ Swedish Bo on Rye /

x 20 canapés,
more or less

Preparation: 30 minutes

Ingredients

- 1 loaf rye bread, preferably small in diameter
- 6 or 7 smoked herring fillets
- 2 small sweet onion
- 2 handfuls black or green grapes
- 1 handful red currants
- ½ untreated lemon
- 40 g/1½ oz/2⅔ tablespoons softened butter
- 2 tablespoons raspberry jam
- a few sprigs parsley
- olive oil
- salt and pepper

Cut 20 slices of rye bread in the shape and size of your choice. Toast them. Butter them lightly and spread them with a little raspberry jam. Season with salt and pepper.

Peel the onion and chop finely. Wash the grapes and the lemon. Cut the grapes into slices and remove the seeds. Cut the lemon into thin sections. Cut the herring fillets into small pieces, removing any bones.

Top the toasts with a little onion, grape and a few pieces of herring. Garnish with red currants, sprinkle with a few drops of olive oil and decorate with a small lemon section and a parsley leaf.

/ The advantage of using organically grown lemons is that you can eat the skin! /

/ A special dedication to my Swedish friend Bo Masser. /

x 2

/ Caribbean-style Niçois /

Preparation: 25 minutes
Cooking time: 30 minutes

Ingredients

- 2 small round bread rolls
- 1 egg
- 2 potatoes
- 4 cherry tomatoes
- 1 handful green beans
- 1 lettuce heart
- 4 dried tomatoes marinated in olive oil
- a few anchovy fillets
- 1 piece strong Caribbean red chilli
- grated coconut
- a few pitted black and green olives
- juice of ½ lemon
- olive oil
- salt and white pepper

Peel the potatoes and cook them in boiling salted water. After 10 minutes, add the green beans and cook another 10 minutes. Hard boil the egg in boiling water for 9 minutes. Refresh under cold water and remove the shell.

Stir the green beans with the chopped dried tomatoes and a little finely chopped chilli, adding a dash of lemon juice, a dash of olive oil and pepper. Cut the potatoes into slices. Wash the lettuce and the tomatoes.

Slice open the bread rolls. Start with a layer of lettuce leaves. Spread with the green bean mixture. Top with a few slices of potatoes and the anchovy fillets. Cut the hard-boiled egg into slices and add them to the sandwiches. Add two or three olives and slices of cherry tomatoes. Sprinkle with grated coconut and olive oil.

/ A Niçoise salad is made with hard-boiled eggs, anchovies and olives. Here we add a little coconut and chilli to give a Caribbean flavour to it. /

x 2

/ Russian Baguette /

Preparation: 30 minutes
Cooking time: 20 minutes

Ingredients

- 1 baguette
- 50 g/1¾ oz fresh shrimp
  (or cooked and frozen)
- 50 g/1¾ oz crab meat
- 1 handful green beans
- 1 potato
- 1 lettuce heart
- 1 small cucumber
- 2 sweet peppers
- 2 large pickles
- 1 bunch parsley
- 2 tablespoons creamy yogurt
- olive oil
- salt and pepper

If you are using fresh shrimp, drop them into boiling salted water, bring back to a boil, drain and shell. If they are frozen, allow them to thaw slowly to room temperature and then shell them. Peel the potatoes and cook them in boiling salted water. After 10 minutes, add the green beans and cook another 10 minutes.

Peel the cucumber and grate three-quarters of it. Wash the lettuce. Cut the baguette into two and then each piece lengthwise. Spread both the top and bottom with grated cucumber. Cut the green beans into pieces.

Mix together the shrimp, the crab, the green beans and the yogurt. Season with salt, pepper and a handful of chopped parsley. Add a few potato slices to each sandwich and then add the shrimp mixture. Top with a few pieces of cucumber, the pickles, the chilli, a few lettuce leaves and parsley. Sprinkle with olive oil.

x 4

/ Jura Burger /

Preparation: 35 minutes
Cooking time: 5 minutes

Ingredients

- 4 small round bread rolls
  or hamburger buns
- 600 to 800 g/1 lb 5 oz to 1¾ lb lean
  ground beef
- 100 to 150 g/3½ to 5¼ oz comté
  cheese
- 6 small carrots
- a few leaves salad greens
- juice of ½ lemon
- olive oil
- white pepper

Mayonnaise:
- 4 dried tomatoes marinated in olive oil
- 6 to 8 gherkins
- 1 egg yolk, at room temperature
- 1 tablespoon mustard
- 1 teaspoon honey
- 1 teaspoon red wine vinegar
- 15 cl/5 fl oz/⅗ cup sunflower oil
- 5 cl/1¾ fl oz/¼ cup olive oil
- salt and white pepper

Mix the egg yolk, mustard and vinegar. Season with salt and pepper. Add the oil little by little, whisking constantly to make the mayonnaise. Chop the dried tomatoes and the gherkins, and add them to the mayonnaise. Season with salt and pepper. Add the honey and mix well.

Peel the carrots and grate them (medium grater), then add the lemon juice. Grate the cheese. Wash the salad greens.

Cut open the bread rolls or buns and toast them under the broiler. Shape the ground beef into patties. Cook them in a hot skillet with a little oil (this sandwich is very good with rare or very rare hamburgers).

Divide up the grated carrots onto the bread rolls, top with a hamburger patty, a few salad greens, followed by more carrots, and finally the grated comté cheese. Season with pepper. Serve the burgers with the mayonnaise.

/ Mini 'wiches /

Preparation: 15 minutes

Ingredients

- 8 slices white bread
- 4 smoked, peppered mackerel fillets
- 3 or 4 carrots
- a few sprigs parsley
- 1 teaspoon curry paste
  (Asian specialty stores)
- 30 g/1 oz/2 tablespoons softened
  butter
- juice of ½ lemon
- olive oil
- salt and black pepper

Toast the bread slices. Remove the crust. Mix the softened butter with the curry paste to taste. Spread this mixture on the slices of bread.

Peel the carrots and make some strips using a vegetable peeler. Grate the remaining carrots, add the chopped parsley, sprinkle with lemon juice and olive oil and season with salt and pepper. Divide the grated carrots up and spread onto half of the bread slices.

Cut the mackerel fillets into small pieces and add them to the toasts. Cover each with another slice of bread. Cut each sandwich into four small squares. Decorate with a strip of carrot and a parsley leaf. Sprinkle with a little olive oil. Season with salt and pepper.

x 2

/ Camembert Croque /

Preparation: 15 minutes
Cooking time: 5 minutes

Ingredients

- 4 slices white bread (sized to fit a French croque-monsieur press)
- ½ camembert
- 1 small sweet onion
- 1 firm, white mushroom
- a few leaves salad greens
- 25 g to 30 g/about 1 oz/about 2 table-spoons butter
- red wine vinegar

Remove the stem from the mushroom and slice the cap thinly. Peel the onion and chop it. Cut the camembert half into six portions.

Butter the bread, place two slices in croque-monsieur press, buttered side facing the press. Top one slice with mushroom slices and onion, half the camembert and again some mushroom slices and onion. Sprinkle with a little vinegar.

Close the croque press without tightening it completely and place over a medium gas flame. Turn over every minute, cooking until the croque is golden. Serve hot on a bed of salad greens.

/ If you do not have a croque-monsieur press, you can make the croques with a panini press or an electric sandwich or croque-monsieur toaster. You can also make them in the oven, preheated to 200°C/400°F/gas 7, and finish them off under the broiler. In this case, the croque will not be pressed. /

/ Turkey to You Too! /

Preparation: 30 minutes
Cooking time: 1 minute

Ingredients

- 1 olive baguette
- 500 to 600 g/1 lb 2 oz to 1 lb 5 oz turkey or other poultry liver
- 200 g/7 oz/¾ cup cooked chickpeas
- 4 or 5 tablespoons pesto
- 1 small little gem butterhead lettuce or 1 mini lettuce
- a few pitted black olives
- 1 lump butter
- juice of ½ lemon
- sunflower oil
- olive oil
- salt and pepper

Heat a skillet or a pot with a dash of sunflower oil and a lump of butter. Brown the turkey livers 30 seconds on each side, over a high heat. Remove from heat, cover and set aside. The liver should remain slightly pink inside.

Cut the baguette into slices diagonally. Spread each slice with pesto. Season the chickpeas with olive oil, lemon juice, salt and pepper. Crush them roughly with a fork and spread the mixture onto the bread.

Cut the liver into slices and place a slice on each canapé. Sprinkle with olive oil. Wash the lettuce leave and cut into thin strips. Season with a little olive oil and divide up among the canapés. Cut the olives into slices and use them to decorate the canapés.

x 2

/ Tuna Croque /

Preparation: 15 minutes
Cooking time: 5 minutes

Ingredients

- 4 slices white bread (sized to fit in a French croque-monsieur press)
- 60 g/2 oz tuna (canned, in water, or fresh and cooked)
- 1 small onion or shallot
- 1 tomato
- 1 spring onion or a few branches of parsley
- 25 to 30 g/1½ to 2 tablespoons butter (sweet or salted)
- olive oil
- red wine vinegar
- salt and white pepper

Peel the onion, wash the tomato, and cut both into a small dice. Peel the spring onion and chop. Mix all the above with the flaked tuna. Season with salt and pepper and sprinkle with a dash of olive oil and a few drops of vinegar.

Butter the bread, place two slices in croque-monsieur press, buttered side facing the press. Add the tuna mixture, close the croque press without tightening it completely and place over a medium gas heat. Turn over every minute, cooking until the croque is golden. Serve hot.

x 2

/ Europa Kebab /

Preparation: 30 minutes
Cooking time: 25 minutes

Ingredients

- 1 baguette
- 200 to 300 g/7 to 10½ oz ground lamb
- 1 aubergine (eggplant)
- 1 firm, white mushroom
- 1 tomato
- ½ cucumber
- a few leaves salad greens
- 1 bunch coriander leaves (cilantro)
- 1 red or green chilli
- 1 lemon
- 2 tablespoons creamy yogurt
- 1 teaspoon ground cumin
- olive oil
- salt and pepper

Preheat the oven to 240°C/475°F/gas 9. Wash all the vegetables. Cut the aubergine in half lengthwise. Bake the half aubergines in the oven for 20 minutes, until they are well cooked.

Remove the stem from the mushroom, cut the cap into thin slices, and sprinkle with a little lemon juice. Peel the cucumber and cut it into thin slices.

Sprinkle the meat with the ground cumin, salt and pepper. Shape two, oval patties. Brown them in a lightly oiled, very hot skillet, for a few minutes.

Cut the baguette into two and then each piece open lengthwise. Grate the tomato over the bread and spread the pulp. Place a few salad greens in the sandwich, along with some cucumber slices. Remove the flesh of the aubergine from the skin and add it to the sandwiches. Add the mushrooms and then the meat. Sprinkle with olive oil. Finish with a touch of yogurt and some coriander leaves. Season with pepper.

Serve with the chilli and, if you want, a lemon section.

/ This kebab-style sandwich can made with semolina bread or pita bread. /

x 1

/ Sea Scallop Mezze /

Preparation: 15 minutes
Cooking time: 7 minutes

Ingredients

- 1 panini roll
- 4 or 6 sea scallops
- 2 tablespoons cooked chickpeas
  + a few for the salad
- 1 handful whole almonds
- 1 generous teaspoon cumin seeds
- 1 small bunch fresh coriander leaves
- 1 handful rocket
- juice of ½ lemon
- olive oil
- salt and pepper

If you buy whole sea scallops, shell them, remove the beard and the coral (you can save the latter for another preparation). Wash the scallops by placing them in a large quantity of water and lifting them out, three times, without allowing them to soak. Cut each scallop in two and place in a small bowl. Add the chickpeas, sprinkle with lemon juice and a dash of olive oil. Season with salt and pepper. Chop the almonds roughly. Chop the coriander leaves. Add both to the preparation. Sprinkle with cumin seeds.

Cut open the panini roll. Sprinkle the inside with olive oil. Garnish with the sea scallop mixture. Close the sandwich with the top and cook in a panini or sandwich press for about 7 minutes. Serve on a bed of rocket, sprinkled with a few chickpeas.

/ This recipe is an encounter between Brittany and Lebanon, with an original marriage of sea scallops, chickpeas, cumin and coriander. /

x 4

/ Brazil-style Halal /

Preparation: 30 minutes

Ingredients

- 1 round semolina bread
- 12 very thin slices cooked chicken or chicken breast
- 2 avocados
- 1 courgette (zucchini)
- 1 handful almonds and Brazil nuts
- a few sprigs fresh mint
- a few fennel tops
- 1 touch harissa spice paste (optional)
- juice of ½ lemon
- olive oil
- salt and pepper

Chop the almonds and Brazil nuts in a food processor. Peel the avocados, crush with a fork, add a dash of olive oil, salt, pepper and, if you like, a touch of harissa. Wash the courgette and cut into very thin slices using a vegetable peeler or a mandoline (see page 26). Sprinkle with lemon juice, salt and pepper. Cut the bread into slices and toash them in the oven or a toaster. Spread each slice with the mashed avocado.

Roll up the chicken slices and then cut into slices. Place them on the avocado. Add the lemoned courgettes. Sprinkle with the almond and Brazil nut mixture. Add a few sprigs of fennel tops and a little chopped fresh mint. Top off with a dash of olive oil and a little pepper.

/ Brazil nuts are very rich (full of fatty acids and minerals, among other things), and as a result, they make an interesting supplement to a balanced diet when eaten with moderation. /

x 2

/ Celtic Lebanese /

Preparation: 25 minutes
Cooking time: 10 minutes

Ingredients

- 2 thick slices rye bread
- 2 cod fillets, 4¼ oz each
- 8 green asparagus
- 4 or 5 tablespoons cooked chickpeas
- 1 firm, white mushroom
- 1 lemon + juice of ½ lemon
- a few sprigs of parsley
- 1 egg
- 1 bowl flour
- 1 bowl dried breadcrumbs
- olive oil
- salt and pepper

Cut off the hard part of the asparagus stems, and peel the rest. Slice them diagonally, keeping the tips whole. Heat a skillet over high heat, add olive oil and the asparagus, salt and pepper. Cover and cook over low heat for 3 to 4 minutes. Prepare a bowl of flour; another bowl with the beaten egg and chopped parsley, salt and pepper; and a final bowl with dried breadcrumbs. Trim the cod fillets into more or less rectangular steaks. Coat them first in the flour, then the egg and finally the breadcrumbs. Heat a dash of oil in a hot skillet and brown the breaded fish, 2 minutes on each side.

Finely slice the mushroom cap. Place the chickpeas in a bowl, sprinkle with a dash of olive oil and season with salt and pepper. Crush the roughly, and then add the sliced mushroom. Sprinkle with lemon juice and mix.

Spread this chickpea and mushroom mixture onto the two thick slices of rye bread. Top with the breaded cod, followed by the grilled asparagus. Wedge the asparagus tips under the breaded cod. Peel the lemon, removing the pith and the white membranes. Cut into thin slices and place them on either side of the fish. Decorate with a sprig of parsley.

/ Rye is a grain that grows in poor soil and low temperatures, and it has been popular for centuries, and even for millennia in certain countries. In France, it was all but forgotten in favour of wheat flour in the twentieth century (when white bread was no longer a luxury), yet its strong flavour is very appreciated. /

x 2

/ Italian-American Trucker's Sandwich /

Preparation: 25 minutes
Cooking time: 25 minutes

Ingredients

- ½ loaf long bread
- 2 chicken or turkey escalopes
- 2 or 3 potatoes
- 1 large shallot
- 1 spring onion
- a few cherry tomatoes
- 1 tablespoon dried herbs (marjoram, basil, etc.)
- juice of ½ orange
- juice of ½ lemon
- olive oil
- sunflower oil
- salt and pepper

Cut the bread into two and cut open the two pieces for sandwiches. Toast them in the oven or toaster. Flatten the chicken or turkey with a heavy utensil. Sprinkle them with dried herbs and brown them in a skillet for a few minutes, with a little olive oil.

Peel the potatoes and grate them. Season with salt and pepper. Place two piles of grated potatoes in a skillet with a dash of sunflower oil and cook over medium heat, pressing them flat with a wooden spoon (or use a small, individual skillet and make to potato pancakes one by one). Cover and cook for about 15 minutes.

Peel the shallot and the spring onion. Slice them, season with olive oil and lemon juice, salt and pepper. Slice the cooked chicken and sprinkle with orange juice and a dash of olive oil. Place a potato pancake in the sandwich. Add the chicken and the shallot and spring onion mixture. Serve with cherry tomatoes.

/ Flattening the escalopes by pounding them with a heavy utensil (a heavy skillet, a heavy knife, a rolling pin, etc.) partially breaks down the fibres, making the meat more tender, and makes them thinner, evening out the thickness. /

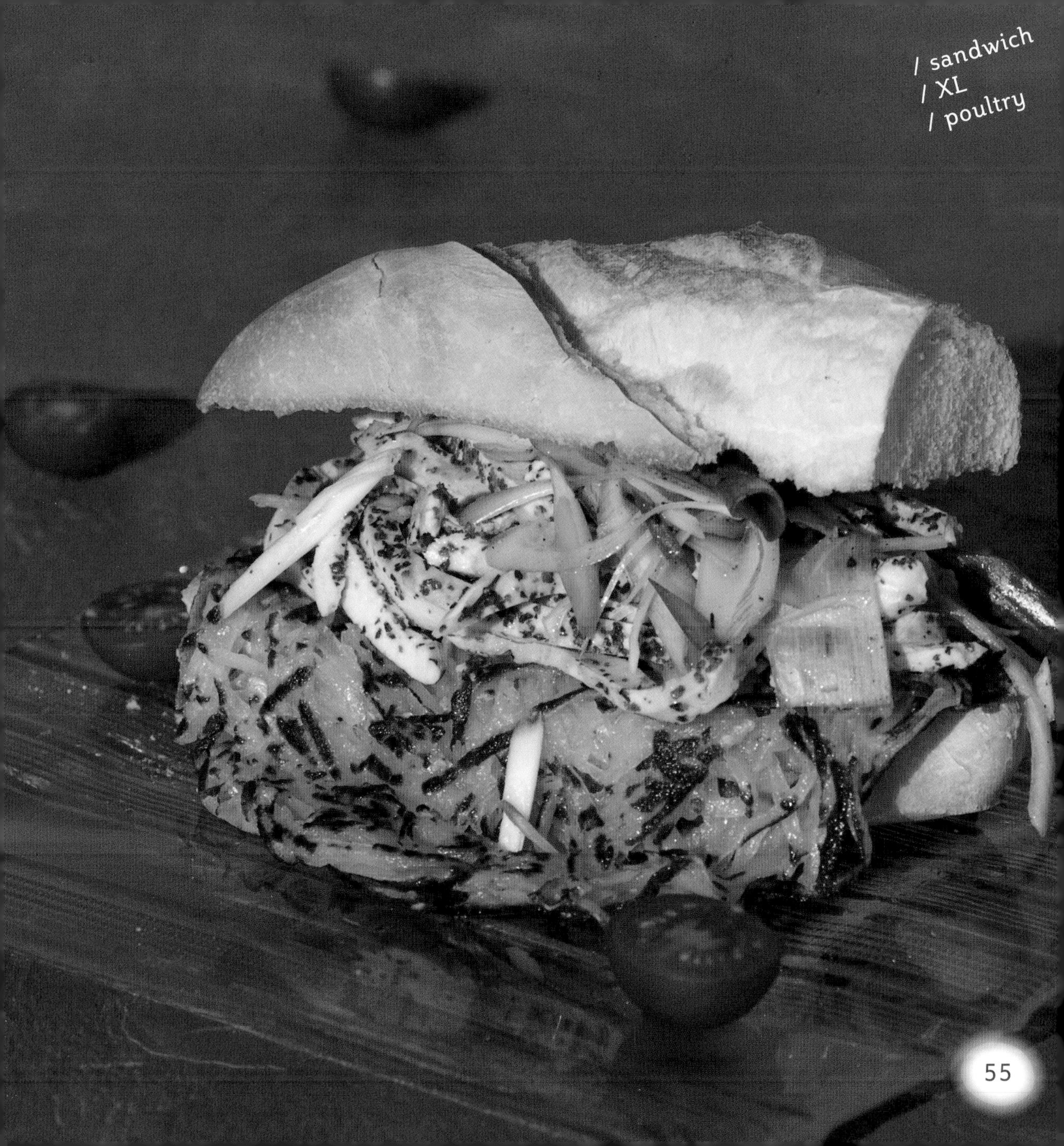
/ sandwich
/ XL
/ poultry

x 1

/ Cretan Flavours /

Preparation: 15 minutes
Cooking time: 20 minutes

Ingredients

- 3 slices multi-grain bread
- 1 aubergine (eggplant)
- 1 handful young spinach leaves
- 1 cherry tomatoes
- 50 to 70 g/1¾ to 2½ oz/about ⅓ cup feta
- 3 tablespoons creamy yogurt
- 1 handful black olives
- juice of ½ lemon
- juice of ½ orange
- olive oil
- salt and pepper

Preheat the oven to 240°C/475°F/gas 9. Cut the aubergine in half lengthwise. Bake the half aubergines in the oven for 20 minutes, until they are well cooked. Remove the skin and cut into large pieces. Salt. Dice the feta. Wash the spinach. Sprinkle a slice of bread with olive oil. Top with a few raw spinach leaves, a few pieces of aubergine, olives and some feta. Sprinkle with lemon juice and orange juice. Add a tablespoon of yogurt and season with pepper. Repeat to make two further layers. Top with a cherry tomato.

/ This layered open sandwich whisks you away to Crete... /

x 1

/ Oriental Special /

Preparation: 25 minutes
Cooking time: 20 minutes

Ingredients

- ½ round loaf barley bread
- 3 thin slices pastrami (see page 20)
- 1 red bell pepper
- ½ tomato
- a few black olives
- a few gherkins
- a few pickled sweet peppers (optional)
- 1 clove garlic
- 1 small bunch fresh coriander leaves (cilantro) or parsley
- 1 handful almonds and Brazil nuts
- juice of ½ lemon
- olive oil

Preheat the oven to 240°C/475°F/gas 9. Put the bell pepper on a baking dish and grill it in the oven for about 20 minutes, turning it so that all the sides are grilled. Allow to cool and remove the skin.

Slice off the rounded end of the half-loaf of bread so that it will stand on its end. Remove the better portion of the inside, crumble it and dry under the broiler for 1 to 2 minutes.

Chop the almonds and Brazil nuts in a food processor. Chop the coriander leaves, peel the garlic and chop finely.

Wash the half tomato and grate it to recuperate the pulp. Add the coriander, garlic and a generous tablespoon of chopped almonds and Brazil nuts. Sprinkle with a dash of olive oil and lemon juice. Chop the pepper and pickles peppers, adding them to the above mixture along with 2 handfuls of dried breadcrumbs. Cut the pastrami into very thin strips. Garnish the bread with the pepper mixture, and top with the pastrami strips. Sprinkle with olive oil and add a few olives and a little chopped coriander leaves. Sprinkle with almonds and Brazil nuts. Decorate with a sweet pepper and a gherkin.

x 1

/ Indian Special /

Preparation: 15 minutes
Cooking time: 12 minutes

Ingredients

- 1 panini roll
- 1 chicken breast
- 2 or 3 fresh pineapple slices
- a few mung bean sprouts
- a few sprigs of parsley
- a few small pickled green chillies
- 1 small teaspoon of each of the following spices: cardamom, garam masala, curcuma, white pepper
- olive oil
- salt

Heat a small cast-iron pot. Mix the spices well and sprinkle on the chicken breast. Brown both sides in the pot, without any fat (blackening, see page 28), and then cook over a low heat, covered, for about 5 minutes. Wash the bean sprouts and the parsley. Cut open the panini roll. Place some bean sprouts on the bottom slice and a few parsley leaves. Top with the blackened chicken breast. Add a few pieces of pineapple. Sprinkle with olive oil and season with salt. Close the sandwich with the top and cook in a panini or sandwich press for about 7 minutes. Serve with the pickled chillies.

/ Curcuma gives this panini an Indian flavour and a pretty golden colour. /

/ Mung bean sprouts are commonly referred to as "bean sprouts". Mung beans (*Vigna Radiata*) are different from soya beans (*Glycine Max*), which are used to make tofu, soy drinks and the like. Sometimes mung beans are referred to as green soy, by they do not have the protein or reputation of soya beans. Their nutritional value is closer to that of a green vegetable. /

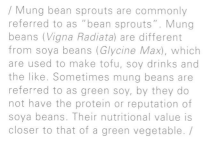

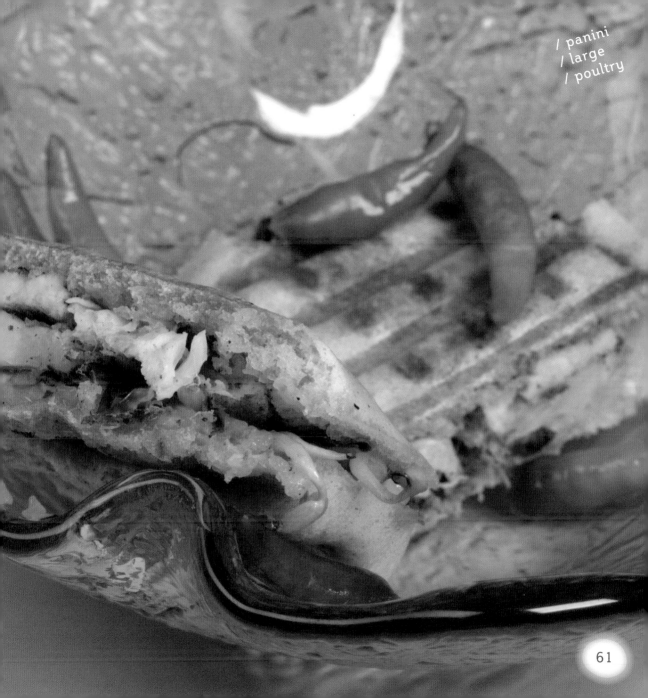

/ Trout Forever /

Preparation: 30 minutes

Ingredients

- 1 loaf whole wheat bread
- 10 or so slices smoked trout
- 1 small little gem butterhead lettuce
- 1 *fromage frais* or sheep's milk yogurt
- 25 to 30 g/1 oz/2 tablespoons softened butter
- 20 or so hard-boiled quail eggs (available already cooked and peeled in jars)
- 2 to 3 tablespoons of sweet and spicy Savora mustard sauce
- a few pinches of curcuma
- salt and pepper

Slice the whole wheat bread and toast. Use a cutter to cut out small canapés from the bread slices. Wash the lettuce and cut the most tender leaves into strips. Cut the smoked trout slices into strips. Cut the quail eggs into four and sprinkle with curcuma. Mix the softened butter with the Savora sauce. Spread this mixture onto the canapés. Top with a little lettuce. Roll up one or two strips of smoked trout and place on the canapé. Top with a teaspoon of sheep's milk yogurt. Add a few quail eggs and season with salt and pepper.

/ There's nothing like smoked trout for a change from salmon! It marries well with the sheep's milk yogurt and makes for tangy mouthfuls, sure to please! /

x 4

/ Alsatian Springtime /

Preparation: 25 minutes
Cooking time: 9 minutes

Ingredients

- 1 loaf corn bread
- 4 slices cooked chicken
- 2 eggs
- 1 courgette (zucchini)
- 1 grapefruit
- 20 or so tinned asparagus, or fresh and cooked
- 1 small bunch mint
- 1 large pinch dill seeds
- olive oil
- salt and pepper

Hard boil the egg in boiling water for 9 minutes. Refresh under cold water and then peel.

Wash the courgette and cut into very thin strips, lengthwise, using a vegetable peeler. Add the dill, season with salt and pepper and sprinkle with olive oil. Peel the grapefruit removing the pith and the outside white membranes. Cut into thin slices.

Cut eight thin slices of corn bread. On four of them, place a few courgette strips, a few mint leaves and a grapefruit slice. Place a slice of cooked chicken over the edge of the sandwich, top with four asparagus and a half a hard-boiled egg, cut into slices. Fold over the slice of cooked chicken and add another strip of courgette and a few mint leaves. Cover with a second slice of bread and, if you want, cut smaller sandwiches. Decorate with an asparagus, a half-slice of grapefruit and a mint leaf.

/ You can use either white or green asparagus for this sandwich. /

x 2

/ Bistro-style Beef /

Preparation: 20 minutes
Cooking time: 3 minutes

Ingredients

- 1 baguette
- 250 g/9 oz beef sirloin
- 4 to 6 portions Laughing Cow spreadable cheese
- 2 carrots
- 1 courgette (zucchini)
- ½ onion
- 1 small bunch parsley
- ½ lemon
- salt and pepper

Heat a slightly oiled skillet over high heat and brown the sirloin on both sides. Season with salt and pepper immediately after removing it from the heat. Set aside.

Wash and chop the parsley. Add it to a bowl with the Laughing Cow and mix with a fork. Peel the carrots and onion. Wash the courgette. Grate these vegetables and mix them together.

Cut the baguette into two and then each piece lengthwise. Place half the vegetable mixture on the bottom pieces. Spread the Laughing Cow and parsley mixture on the tops. Cut the meat into strips and lay out on the vegetables. Sprinkle with a few drops of lemon. Close the sandwich.

/ Sirloin is best rare or medium rare, unless you really like your meat well cooked. You can also use a long, half-cooked bread and make this like a panini. If you do, barely brown the meat for a few seconds; it will finish cooking in the panini press. /

x 2

/ Caribbean Curry Salmon /

Preparation: 30 minutes
Cooking time: 8 minutes

Ingredients

- 1 white or country-style bread
- 2 fillets salmon, 80 to 100 g/3 to 3½ oz each
- ½ head little gem butterhead lettuce
- 4 cherry tomatoes
- ½ Granny Smith apple
- 1 handful pine nuts
- a few sprigs of parsley
- 1 teaspoon Caribbean curry powder
- olive oil
- salt and pepper

Brown the pine nuts under the broiler or in a skillet until golden brown.

Heat a drop of olive oil until hot in a skillet and add the cherry tomatoes to seize them. Cover and cook 3 to 4 minutes, and then remove the skin, which will have opened up. Wash the lettuce and cut into thin strips. Peel the apple half and cut it into a small dice. Add a little chopped parsley, season with salt and pepper and sprinkle with olive oil. Cut the salmon into cubes, add the Caribbean curry powder and a dash of olive oil. Season with salt and pepper. Heat a skillet until very hot and seize the salmon dice for about 1 minute.

Cut two thick slices of bread and toast them in the oven or a toaster. Crush a cherry tomato on each of the bread slices, add a little lettuce, the salmon and the parsleyed apple. Add a few pine nuts and top with the remaining tomato cut in half. Sprinkle with olive oil.

/ You can make these open sandwiches either with white bread, cutting the slices diagonally, or on a large country-style bread cut into large, rather thin slices. /

x 2

/ Baby 'wiches /

Preparation: 10 minutes

Ingredients

- 1 small cheese baguette
- 2 Babybel or other hard cheese
- 2 or 3 cherry tomatoes
- a few lettuce leaves
- ½ kiwi
- olive oil
- salt

Cut the baguette into two and then each piece lengthwise. Peel the kiwi, cut in two, top to bottom, and then each half in slices. Wash the tomatoes and cut them into small sections. Wash the lettuce leaves and chop roughly. Cut the Babybel into slices. Layer the bottom slice of bread with lettuce. Top with cheese, kiwi and tomato. Salt lightly and sprinkle with a dash of olive oil. Close the sandwiches.

/ These are small, fun sandwiches. If possible, choose a cheese baguette with a soft inside that is brioche-like, or choose a *fougasse*, if you find one with more inside than crust. /

x 1

/ Mega Beef Open /

Preparation: 30 minutes
Cooking time: 4 minutes

Ingredients

- 1 small round bread
- 150 to 200 g/5¼ to 7 oz beef sirloin
- 1 cooked artichoke heart (see page 18)
- 1 head little gem butterhead lettuce
- 1 small tomato
- 1 cherry tomato for decoration
- ½ small sweet onion
- a few sprigs of parsley
- 1 teaspoon ground cumin
- 1 pinch cumin seeds
- sunflower oil
- olive oil
- salt and pepper

Cut the sirloin into slices. Add the ground cumin, cumin seeds, salt and pepper and mix well.

Peel and slice the onion. Wash the lettuce and cut the leaves lengthwise into strips. Cut the artichoke heart into slices. Wash the parsley and tomato. Chop the parsley finely. Cut the tomato into thin slices.

Cut the top off the bread loaf, like a hat. Toast the bottom in the oven. Heat a skillet with a dash of sunflower oil. Add the lettuce and the onion and cook over high heat for 1 minute, without stirring. Cook for one more minute, sautéing the vegetables.

On the bread, layer tomato slices, a few slices of artichoke and the chopped parsley. Salt. Top with the lettuce and onion.

In a very hot skillet without oil, brown the meat for 1 minute, stirring regularly. Put the meat on the vegetables. Add the remaining artichoke. Decorate with a cherry tomato cut into sections. Sprinkle with a little olive oil and salt.

x 4

/ Open-face Chicken Melt /

Preparation: 35 minutes
Cooking time: 15 minutes

Ingredients

- 1 sesame bread
- 4 slices cooked chicken
- 1 courgette (zucchini)
- 4 firm, white mushrooms
- 60 g/2 oz emmental cheese
- 30 g/1 oz/2 tablespoons salt butter
- a few sprigs of parsley
- juice of ½ lemon
- salt and pepper

White sauce:
- 1 tablespoon of butter
- 1 scant tablespoon flour
- 50 g/1¾ oz emmental cheese
- 1 pinch ground nutmeg
- 25 cl/9 fl oz/1 cup milk
- salt and pepper

Prepare the white sauce: melt the butter over low heat and whisk in the flour. Pour in the milk little by little, whisking continuously. Season with nutmeg, salt and pepper. Remove from heat when the sauce has thickened. Grate the emmental, add to the white sauce and mix. Add more milk if you find the sauce too thick.

Preheat the oven to 220°C/425°F/gas 8. Cut the chicken into thin strips; grate the emmental. Wash the courgette and slice into tagliatelle-sized strips using a vegetable peeler. Remove the stems from the mushrooms and slice the caps thinly. Place around one third of these vegetables onto a plate, add the chopped parsley, salt, pepper and sprinkle with lemon juice.

Cut four thick slices of sesame bread. Spread them with salt butter, place in a baking dish and brown them for a few minutes in the oven. Cover with cooked chicken, courgette and mushrooms. Spread with a generous quantity of white sauce and cover with grated emmental. Bake for 7 to 8 minutes. Serve these melts on a bed of courgette-mushroom salad.

x 2

/ Smokin' Mozza–Cod Liver Special /

Preparation: 10 minutes

Ingredients

- 2 slices bread
- 100 g/3½ oz smoked cod liver
- 1 mozzarella (the real thing, made with buffalo milk)
- 4 cherry or olivette tomatoes
- ½ Granny Smith apple
- a few pinches dried basil or a few fresh leaves
- juice of ½ lemon
- olive oil
- salt and pepper

Toast the bread slices in the oven. Peel the apple half and cut it into sticks. Sprinkle these with lemon juice. Wash the cherry tomatoes and cut into quarters. Cut the mozzarella into half-slices. Top the toasts with tomato quarters, apple sticks, and pieces of mozzarella. Add pieces of the smoked cod liver. Season with salt and pepper and sprinkle with a little olive oil. Decorate with dry or fresh basil.

/ Oh, that infamous cod-liver oil our mothers gave us so we would grow up faster! They were right to do so, because cod liver contain numerous nutrients. In the nineteenth century, a campaign promoted it to prevent rickets. Here is a nourishing sandwich, which uses the whole livers rather than just the oil. /

/ Yummy Quail /

Preparation: 30 minutes
Cooking time: 1 minute

Ingredients

- 20 slices round white bread
- 20 very fresh quail eggs, at room temperature
- a few mung bean sprouts (see page 60)
- 1 handful rocket
- 2 slices pickled ginger (Asian specialty stores)
- a few bunches of red currants
- 40 g/1½ oz/2⅔ tbsp softened butter (or mayonnaise)
- 1 dash curcuma
- white vinegar
- salt and black pepper

Use a knife to break the quail eggs delicately into a small recipient. Prepare a bowl of cold water. Heat a large pot with 2 to 3 cm (about 1 in) water mixed with some white vinegar (do not use too much water to make the poached eggs, or else they do not shape properly). When the water is simmering, pour the eggs in one at a time and cook for barely a minute. Remove the eggs with a skimmer and place them in the bowl of cold water to stop the cooking. Set aside on a small plate.

Cut strips of pickled ginger. Wash the lettuce and the bean sprouts (cut the sprouts in two if they are very long). If you want to, remove the crust from the bread using a biscuit cutter. Spread the bread slices with butter, top with a few rocket leaves and a few bean sprouts. Add a poached quail egg. Surround the egg with small strips of pickled ginger and a few red currants. Season with salt, pepper and curcuma.

/ To poach eggs correctly, they need to be very fresh, otherwise the white will not hold and form a smooth round shape. /

x 1

/ Chicken Club /

Preparation: 30 minutes
Cooking time: 15 minutes

Ingredients

- 2 slices of a large loaf white bread
- 1 chicken escalope weighing about 120 g/4¼ oz
- 1 small head broccoli
- 1 tomato
- 1 egg
- 1 small teaspoon curry powder
- 1 small teaspoon sweet paprika
- olive oil
- salt and pepper

Mayonnaise:
- 4 dried tomatoes marinated in olive oil
- 6 to 8 gherkins
- 1 egg yolk, at room temperature
- 1 tablespoon mustard
- 1 teaspoon honey
- 1 teaspoon red wine vinegar
- 15 cl/5 fl oz/⅗ cup sunflower oil
- 5 cl/1¾ fl oz/¼ cup olive oil
- salt and white pepper

Mix the egg yolk, mustard and vinegar. Season with salt and pepper. Add the oil little by little, whisking constantly to make the mayonnaise. Chop the dried tomatoes and the gherkins, and add them to the mayonnaise. Season with salt and pepper. Add the honey and mix well.

Cook the broccoli in salted boiling water for 10 minutes and drain.

Flatten the escalope with a heavy utensil (see page 54). Sprinkle with curry powder and paprika. Brown the chicken for a few minutes in a little olive oil in a skillet. Toast the bread slices. Slice the chicken and the broccoli. Wash the tomato and cut into thin slices.

Spread a little mayonnaise on each slice of bread. Top with a few pieces of chicken, add a little mayonnaise and some broccoli. Repeat for two more layers. Finish with tomato slices and a dash of olive oil. Season with pepper. Cut the sandwich in two, diagonally, to make two club sandwiches. Fry an egg, season with salt and serve with the sandwich.

x 1

/ The Violet /

Preparation: 25 minutes
Cooking time: 7 minutes

Ingredients

- 1 panini roll
- 2 baby violet artichokes
- 1 handful rocket
- 60 g/2 oz mozzarella (the real thing, made with buffalo milk)
- 5 pitted green olives
- juice of ½ lemon
- 1 pinch dry basil
- olive oil
- salt and white pepper

Remove the large leaves from the artichokes; cut off the pointed tips of the remaining leaves. Cut the artichokes in two, carefully remove the choke, then slice and sprinkle with lemon immediately. Wash the lettuce, add to the artichokes along with the green olives and the dry basil. Sprinkle with olive oil, salt and pepper. Mix well and marinate for 5 minutes.

Cut open the panini roll. Sprinkle the inside with olive oil. Fill the panini with the artichoke mixture. Cut the mozzarella into large slices and place on top of the artichokes. Close the sandwich with the top slice of bread and cook in a panini or sandwich press for about 7 minutes.

x 4

/ Quick Salmon, Quebec Style /

Preparation: 30 minutes

Ingredients

- 1 loaf mixed grain bread
- 100 g/3½ oz salmon fillet
- 4 firm, white mushroom
- 1 small cucumber
- 1 small bunch mint or parsley
- 1 small handful dill seeds
- 1 tablespoon maple syrup
- juice of 1 lemon
- olive oil
- salt and pepper

Place the salmon fillet in the freezer for 15 minutes or set it aside in a bowl of ice cubes, so that it hardens enough to cut it into thin slices. Cut it into very thin slices, like carpaccio. Remove the skin from the mushrooms, if necessary, and cut into thin slices.

Peel the cucumber and cut it into tagliatelle-like strips using a vegetable peeler. Chop a few mint or parsley leave and add them. Sprinkle with lemon juice, salt and pepper. Mix well. Pour the rest of the lemon juice on the salmon. Add a few dill seeds. Sprinkle with a dash of olive oil and maple syrup. Season with salt and pepper. Mix well.

Cut the bread into slices. Place a few mushroom slices on a piece of bread, with some salmon and cucumber. Prepare several open sandwiches and present them piled up. Decorate with a mint or parsley leaf.

/ A little touch of maple syrup is enough to transport you directly to Quebec. You can add layers depending on how hungry you are. /

/ Mango French Toast /

Preparation: 25 minutes
Cooking time: 1 minute

Ingredients

• 1 loaf bread, preferably a little stale
• 1 mango
• 1 or 2 kiwis
• 4 to 6 physalis
• 1 egg
• 1 tablespoon vanilla sugar
• a little icing (confectioner's) sugar
• 1 small glass milk
• sunflower oil

Cut four to six slices of bread. Peel the kiwi and cut them into slices. Cut open the mango, avoiding the pit. Peel it and put a quarter of the fruit into a food processor. Cut the rest into pretty slices, without cutting through one end, so that you can fan them out. Add the vanilla sugar to the mango in the food processor, along with the milk and the egg. Blend and pour into a bowl. Dip the bread slices into this sauce and allow them to soak.

Heat a skillet with a dash of sunflower oil. Place the bread slices into a hot skillet, and cook them 30 seconds on each side. Remove them from the pan and drain on paper towels. Place a few slices of mango on each piece of French toast, along with a few kiwi slices. Open the calyx of the physalis and place it on top of the mango. Sprinkle lightly with icing sugar.

/ The *Physalis* family covers a number of species, not all of which are edible. The fruit are harvested still wrapped in their calyx, which does not open on its own. The calyx protects the fruit and allows it to ripen evenly (in the picture, we have opened it delicately with the tips of our fingers). You can keep physalis up to several months, if you set them out carefully, not touching each other, in a well-ventilated place. /

x 1

/ Banana Meets Red Currant /

Preparation: 25 minutes
Set aside: a few hours
Cooking time: 7 minutes

Ingredients

- 1 panini roll
- 1 ripe banana
- 2 tablespoons red currants
- a few pieces candied lemon peel
- a few mint leaves
- 1 pinch vanilla sugar
- 20 g/⅔ oz/1⅓ tablespoons softened butter

Chocolate spread:
- 200 g/7 oz bittersweet chocolate (70% cacao solids)
- 150 g/5¼ oz/1 cup whole hazelnuts
- 100 g/3½ oz/½ cup brown sugar
- 50 g/1¾ oz/2 tablespoons honey
- 70 g/2½ oz/⅓ cup powdered milk
- 1 tablespoon cocoa powder
- 100 g/3½ oz/½ cup olive oil
- 1 vanilla pod

Make the chocolate spread: Split the vanilla bean, scrape out the seeds with the tip of a knife. Melt the chocolate over a water bath. Pour the olive oil in a food processor with the hazelnuts, the brown sugar, the honey and the vanilla and blend. Add the milk powder little by little, while blending. Add the warm chocolate and the cocoa, and blend. Pour into a jar, allow it to cool for several hours until it hardens.

Peel the banana and cut into slices diagonally. Cut open the panini bread. Butter the lower piece of bread, top with banana slices. Spread with the chocolate spread. Add the red currants and a few small pieces of candied lemon peel. Sprinkle with vanilla sugar and add a few mint leaves. Close the sandwich with the top and cook in a panini or sandwich press for about 7 minutes.

/ This recipe makes about 700 g/1 lb 7 oz chocolate spread, but you need a lot less than that for the paninis. Choose how much you want to use, and keep the rest for snack time. /

x 4

/ Banana Chocolate Melt /

Preparation: 10 minutes
Cooking time: 5 minutes

Ingredients

- 8 slices white bread (sized to fit in a French croque-monsieur press) or sliced brioche
- 1 banana
- 50 to 60 g/1¾ to 2 oz bittersweet chocolate or milk chocolate, to taste
- 2 tablespoons grated coconut
- 1 packet vanilla sugar (optional)
- 60 g/2 oz/3 generous tablespoons butter, preferably salt butter

Grate the chocolate. Peel the banana and dice it. Mix the chocolate, the banana, the coconut and the vanilla sugar.

Butter the bread, place two slices in croque-monsieur press, buttered side facing the press. Add the banana mixture, close the croque press without tightening it completely and place over a medium gas heat. Turn over every minute, cooking until the croque is golden. Serve hot.

x 1

/ Gourmet Treasure Chest /

Preparation: 20 minutes
Cooking time: 5 minutes

Ingredients

- 1 brioche loaf
- 1 slice honeydew melon or other melon
- 4 cherry tomatoes
- 1 stick candied angelica
- a few red and green candied cherries
- a few mint leaves
- a little icing (confectioner's) sugar
- 3 to 4 tablespoons maple syrup

Cut off a large piece of the brioche loaf. Hollow out the soft inside. Toast this chest, along with another slice, in the oven.

Cook the cherry tomatoes with the maple syrup covered over low heat for a few minutes, to candy them. Cut the candied cherries in two, and the candied angelica into thin slices.

Peel the melon slice, remove the seeds and cut into pieces. Place in the brioche chest with half of the cherry tomatoes.

Add a few angelica slices on the edges of the chest, close with a slice of brioche and top with candied cherries. Decorate the plate with the remaining cherry tomatoes, and pour the tomato cooking juice onto the plate. Add a few mint leaves and sprinkle with icing sugar to decorate.

/ A little treasure chest that transforms snack time into something magic! /

x 4

/ Kid Paninis /

Preparation: 10 minutes
Cooking time: 7 minutes

Ingredients

- 4 small panini rolls
- 1 quarter cantaloupe
- 3 or 4 dried apricots
- 1 generous tablespoon grated coconut
- 1 tablespoon apricot jam
- olive oil

Peel the cantaloupe and cut into a dice. Dice the dried apricots as well and mix with the cantaloupe. Add the grated coconut, a dash of olive oil and the apricot jam. Mix well. Cut open the small panini rolls. Garnish with the cantaloupe mixture. Toast the four small paninis in a panini or sandwich toaster for about 7 minutes.

/ This is an ideal snack for children, being both well balanced and delicious. If you are not a fan of olive oil, use softened butter. /

Acknowledgements

Sandwiches have become a staple meal for people on the run! I think about my friends and those close to me who eat sandwiches nearly every day. We are in a hurry, we eat on the go. And the quick, efficient sandwich is an emblem of our contemporary society.

The adventure of writing this book turned my workshop into a street-side stand, with friends coming and going, tasting, eating and sometimes devouring these delicious preparations. I thank Roland, Jean-Pierre, Gilles, Souade, Philippe, Lo, Cath, Rodolphe, Antoine who escaped from nursing studies, my daughter Alta, Laure, Mimi from Marseille, Claude Lebel my cool neighbour, his two daughters, Marion, the florists at Fleurs de Nice, Karim, Krimo, Gisou, Patou, the Rasta druggist, Philippe, Laurent and Zora, Yves, etc.

Thanks go to my publisher, Jean-Pierre Duval, for his odd sense of humour, and of course for his editorial work, which is not always easy with an eccentric author like me. It is neat to have a publisher who supports and develops my ideas. Thank you to Marie-Alexandre, who wrote and witnessed all the recipes, now seconded by Muriel and Anne, who work in a friendly, close team, that is genuine, and full of laughter as well. Fortunately, because heart and shared happiness are keys to creation in my Malmousque workshop. Thank you to Valentin, the musician-photographer… like usual! Such talent! It was a great pleasure to create these beautiful pictures together, so full of truth!

Thanks to my dear mother, Yvette, who supports me unconditionally, providing inspiration full of maternal love… Long live mothers! Thanks to my father for his perspectives, his advice, and above all his work!

Thanks to my friend Édouard Cointreau, without whom I would not be a passionate author of cookery books: you taught me everything, and above all, you were always there when the lonely path was rough. The confidence you had in me and your friendship gave me the wings I have today!

This book is meant to share my happiness with you, that happiness that happens when I create recipes, when I do what I love most: giving life to culinary equations. I am happy to know my recipes are appreciated, shared with friends and family, and particularly with children, who carry the cultural changes for eating well and well-balanced. Many kisses to my daughter Alta, who has lived among the pots since she was born.

Yvan Cadiou, taste sculptor/www.yvancadiou.com

Note: Wasa, Saint-Moret, Savora, Laughing Cow and Babybel are registered trademarks ®.

Editorial director / Marie-Alexandre Perraud
Editing / Muriel Villebrun, Anne Deblois
Graphic design / Maevi Colomina & Romain Pages Publishing
Translation / Anne Trager
Printing and binding / Delo Tiskarna, Slovenia, Europe
First published in French in 2008, by Romain Pages Editions, France.
British Library Cataloguing in Publication Data available.

ISBN no. 978-1-906909-05-5

Romain Pages Publishing
Lincoln House
300 High Holborn
WC1V 7JH - London
United Kingdom
enquiries@romain-pages.co.uk
www.romain-pages.co.uk

Romain Pages Editions
BP 82030
30252 Sommières cedex
France
contact@romain-pages.com
www.romain-pages.com